EVERYDAY

Encouragement

PAMELA McQUADE

BARBOUR
PUBLISHING

© 2006 by Barbour Publishing, Inc.

ISBN 1-59789-435-4

All rights reserved. No part of this publication may be reproduced or transmitted for commercial purposes, except for brief quotations in printed reviews, without written permission of the publisher.

Churches and other noncommercial interests may reproduce portions of this book without the express written permission of Barbour Publishing, provided that the text does not exceed 500 words or 5 percent of the entire book, whichever is less, and that the text is not material quoted from another publisher. When reproducing text from this book, include the following credit line: "From *Spiritual Refreshment for Women: Everyday Encouragement*, published by Barbour Publishing, Inc. Used by permission."

All scripture quotations, unless otherwise indicated, are taken from the HOLY BIBLE, NEW INTERNATIONAL VERSION®. NIV®. Copyright © 1973, 1978, 1984 by International Bible Society. Used by permission of Zondervan. All rights reserved.

Scripture quotations marked NKJV are taken from the New King James Version. Copyright © 1979, 1980, 1982 by Thomas Nelson, Inc. Used by permission. All rights reserved.

Scripture quotations marked NASB are taken from the New American Standard Bible, © 1960, 1962, 1963, 1968, 1971, 1972, 1973, 1975, 1977, 1995 by The Lockman Foundation. Used by permission.

Scripture quotations marked AMP are taken from the Amplified® Bible, © 1954, 1958, 1962, 1964, 1965, 1987 by The Lockman Foundation. Used by permission.

Scripture quotations marked KJV are taken from the King James Version of the Bible.

Cover design by Kirk DouPonce, dogeareddesign.com

Published by Barbour Publishing, Inc., P.O. Box 719, Uhrichsville, Ohio 44683, www.barbourbooks.com

Our mission is to publish and distribute inspirational products offering exceptional value and biblical encouragement to the masses.

Printed in China.
5 4 3 2 1

Contents

Introduction

May our Lord Jesus Christ himself
and God our Father. . .encourage
your hearts and strengthen you.

2 THESSALONIANS 2:16–17

Some days we need a gentle hand
to pick us up and a voice to whisper
encouragement in our ears. Life can be
challenging, and when trials come our
way, we may feel discouraged. But God
does not fail us, no matter what our days
hold. His Word provides comfort for all
our troubles. In these pages, I hope you
will feel the touch of His tender hand
and find strength for each day.

Anger

God's Plan

My dear brothers, take note of this:
Everyone should be quick to listen, slow
to speak and slow to become angry.

JAMES 1:19

———

God gives good advice on anger. Often, if
we listen carefully and hold our tongues, we
don't become angry in the first place. Good
communication forestalls a lot of emotional
trauma. Hurt emotions often cause us to
speak words we regret, simply making the
problem worse. So when we feel tempted
to anger, let's stop, listen, and hold our
tongues for a while. That's God's plan for
more peaceful relationships.

A Prayerful Solution

*I want men everywhere to lift up holy hands in
prayer, without anger or disputing.*

1 TIMOTHY 2:8

Anger becomes a real trap, even for Christians. When we try to settle differences
angrily, we land in big trouble, affecting and
even destroying a whole congregation.
One solution to anger is prayer. It's hard to
stay angry with someone you pray for, even
if that person continues to irritate you. As
God's Spirit works in your heart, you give
the other person a second, a third, or even a
hundred and third chance. In Jesus,
unrighteous anger cannot linger.

Letting Go of Anger

Now the works of the flesh are evident, which are:
adultery. . .idolatry, sorcery, hatred, contentions,
jealousies, outbursts of wrath.

GALATIANS 5:19–20 NKJV

⬥

It's not something we like to hear, but
according to God, anger is right up there
with sins such as adultery and idolatry.
Most of us feel wrathful occasionally. But
if such feelings take hold of our lives and
bitterness results, we fall into sin. When
anger touches our reactions, let's use it as
a warning sign of an issue that requires our
attention. Through wise action and
prayer, it need not control us.

Good Anger

*Be ye angry, and sin not: let not the
sun go down upon your wrath.*

EPHESIANS 4:26 KJV

We have valid reasons for anger when we
see wrongdoing against the innocent.
But God tells us not to let that anger last
long. We need to come to Him in prayer,
consider the issue in Him, and ultimately
leave it in His hands. If we can help cor-
rect the wrong, we should, but letting
ourselves dwell on the situation until we
fume is not an option. Let anger push us
to do good, not ruin our emotional health.

Gentle Speech

A gentle answer turns away wrath,
but a harsh word stirs up anger.

PROVERBS 15:1

How you speak can strongly affect those around you. If someone is hot under the collar, do you quell that anger with calming words or inflame him with harsh ones? Do you start a forest fire with your sister who irritates you or quench the blaze with soft words? Anger's heat makes wise decision making impossible. But God's Word offers advice that brings peace to our lives. Gentle speech leads to wiser choices.

Anxiety

In His Hands

*Do not be anxious about anything, but
in everything, by prayer and petition, with
thanksgiving, present your requests to God.*

PHILIPPIANS 4:6

Need a sure cure for anxiety? Start praying.

As you trust that God has your best interests at

heart, no matter what situation you face, His

peace can replace concern. God says there's

nothing you need to worry about. Just put all

your troubles in His hands, and He who rules

universe upon universe yet knows each hair

on your head will see that everything works out

right. Are you ready to trust now?

Today!

"Therefore do not worry about tomorrow, for tomorrow will worry about itself. Each day has enough trouble of its own."

Matthew 6:34

———

You can look ahead and obsess about fears for the future or take life one day at a time and enjoy it. But you only live in today, not in the weeks, months, and years that may lie ahead. You can only change life in the moment you're in now. Since worry never improves the future and only hurts today, you'll benefit most from trusting in God and enjoying the spot where He's planted you for now.

God Is in Control

*"Who of you by worrying can add
a single hour to his life?"*

MATTHEW 6:27

❦

What does worry gain us? It can't change
the length of our days, except to decrease
the health of our bodies. Ultimately,
worry is the most self-defeating thing we
can engage in. Besides, why should we
give in to concern when God controls our
lives? He will always set us on the right
path, so we don't have to agonize
over life's details.

Sharing with Jesus

Casting all your care upon him;
for he careth for you.

1 PETER 5:7 KJV

———

You don't have a care in the world that you
cannot share—with Jesus, that is. There
isn't one thing He doesn't want to hear
about from you. Before you ask a friend to
pray for you (and you should do that), be
certain you share your care with your best
Friend, Jesus. Your human friend may try to
help you and may do a lot for you, but no one
helps like Jesus. There's no worry
He can't alleviate or remove.

Blessings

Blessing Others

We work hard with our own hands. When we are cursed, we bless; when we are persecuted, we endure it.

God gave Paul many blessings, and the apostle passed them on, even if the recipients didn't seem to really deserve them. Those who cursed him (and they were, no doubt, many) did not receive a cursing in return. Instead, Paul tried to bless them. Do we follow the apostle's example? When we are cursed by the words of others, what is our response?

Powerful Prayer

"The LORD bless you and keep you; the LORD make his face shine upon you and be gracious to you."

NUMBERS 6:24–25

❦

Want to pray for someone? This is a good way to do it. It's the blessing God gave to Aaron and his sons, to pronounce on Israel. What Christian wouldn't appreciate these words, committing her to God's care and wanting her to draw closer to Him? Who would turn down the good things God has to offer? Can you bless your friends and family with these thoughts today?

Living for Christ

If you live according to the sinful nature, you will die; but if by the Spirit you put to death the misdeeds of the body, you will live.

ROMANS 8:13

⬥⬥⬥

Living for Christ through His Spirit offers real life, overflowing and abundant.
Blessings spill over in obedient lives.
But the world, at war with God, doesn't
understand. Unbelievers never feel the
touch of the Spirit in their hearts and
lives, and Jesus' gentle love is foreign to
them. Put to death worldly misdeeds, and
instead of the emptiness of the world,
you'll receive blessings indeed.

Hold on to Hope

The prospect of the righteous is joy, but the
hopes of the wicked come to nothing.

PROVERBS 10:28

⟠

Trusting in Jesus gave you new life and hope
for eternity. So how do you respond when
life becomes dark and dull? Does hope slip
away? When no obviously great spiritual
works are going on, do not assume God has
deserted you. Hold on to Him even more
firmly and trust. He will keep His promises.
Truly, what other option do you have?
Without Him, hope disappears.

An Obedient Life

How blessed are those whose way is blameless,
who walk in the law of the LORD.

PSALM 119:1 NASB

─────◦◦◦◦◦─────

Want to be blessed? Then don't live a sin-
filled life. God can't pour out blessings
on anyone who consistently ignores His
commands. Blessings belong to those who
hear God's Word and take it to heart, living
it out in love. Want to be blessed? Obey the
Master. You'll live blamelessly and joyfully.

Children

Share Your Faith

Train up a child in the way he should go: and
when he is old, he will not depart from it.

PROVERBS 22:6 KJV

What a promise for Christian parents! When
you feel pressured by the task, take comfort.
You are not alone—your Father is with you
and promises that the effective witness of
your life, as you teach your children
His way, will not fail to bless them.
Parents who have just come to Christ
can begin the training today. It is never
too late to share your faith with
those you love most.

A Godly Example

"Let the little children come to Me, and do not forbid them; for of such is the kingdom of heaven."

MATTHEW 19:14 NKJV

⸺

On earth, Jesus loved children. He never shut them out. Though their youth gave them little credence in Israel, He saw the faith potential in them. Certainly the children loved Jesus, too, for His kindheartedness. Do we shut children out of our lives because we are too busy or have more "important" things on our minds? Then we need to take an example from Jesus. For a new take on God's kingdom, spend time with a child today.

The Gift of Children

Sons are a heritage from the LORD,
children a reward from him.

PSALM 127:3

⟨⟨⟨⟩⟩⟩

Today, many people see children more as
a punishment than a reward. But when you
hear of parents who wish they had never
had children, you know they're missing out.
God creates families to love each other and
share His joys. Parents who honestly live
out their faith before their children can also
guide them into a good family life. Are your
children a blessing? He's given them as a
reward, not as a punishment. Do you treat
them that way?

Wise Correction

The rod of correction imparts wisdom, but a
child left to himself disgraces his mother.

PROVERBS 29:15

In today's world, fears of child abuse have
caused us to ignore this verse. Have we
therefore missed the power of correction,
which gives our children wisdom? As God
restrains us from wrongdoing, we need to
stop our children, too. We need not touch a
child physically to modify behavior. Will we
discipline harmful actions now or lose the
chance to be proud of our self-controlled
children who love the Lord?

Comfort

God of Comfort

[God] comforts us in all our troubles, so that we can comfort those in any trouble with the comfort we. . .have received from God.

2 CORINTHIANS 1:4

⸺

When you hurt, God offers you comfort. No trouble is so large or so small that He will not help. But when you have received His strength for the trouble at hand, do you share it in turn? Comfort isn't meant to be hidden away, but passed on to those in a similar need. As part of the body of Christ, we—the church—should be sharing the knowledge that God cares for and strengthens all His children.

Reaching Out

*Just as the sufferings of Christ flow over
into our lives, so also through Christ
our comfort overflows.*

2 Corinthians 1:5

—◆—

Paul knew the pain of persecution, but he
also knew the deep comfort God offered.
When people gave the apostle trouble, God
drew His servant close to His heart. When
trials come your way, God will do the same
for you. If life is always going smoothly,
comfort is meaningless, but when you're
in the midst of trouble, He comes alongside with tender love that overflows your
trials and reaches out to others.

Renewal of Faith

*"As one whom his mother comforts,
so I will comfort you."*

ISAIAH 66:13 NKJV

❧

Like a tender mother, God comforts His
people. When life challenges us, we have a
place to renew our faith. Instead of ques-
tioning God's compassion because we face a
trial, we can draw ever nearer to Him, seeking to do His will. Surrounded by His tender
arms, we gain strength to go out
and face the world again.

Giver of Comfort

*You ought to forgive and comfort him, so that he
will not be overwhelmed by excessive sorrow.*

2 Corinthians 2:7

⸺

Do you know someone who is sorry for her
sin? Then don't keep reminding her of it. If
she has sought forgiveness and put it behind
her, it is dead. Instead of criticizing, remind
her of the power of God that works in her
life. Encourage her when temptation calls
her name. Then she will not be overcome by
sorrow and fall into sin again. Give comfort,
and you will be a blessing.

Contentment

God's Provision

Now godliness with contentment is great gain.

1 TIMOTHY 6:6 NKJV

━━━◆◆◆━━━

Paul warned Timothy against false teachers
who wanted to use the church for financial
gain. If these people were looking for
security, they were on the wrong track.
Money, which comes and goes, never brings
real protection. Our security lies in God's
provision. Whether or not we have a large
bank account, we can feel content in Jesus.
The One who brought us into this world will
never forget we require food, clothing, and
all the rest. When we truly trust in Jesus,
contentment is sure to follow.

Look to the Shepherd

The LORD is my shepherd, I shall not be in want.

PSALM 23:1

❧

No matter what your physical circumstances, if Jesus is your Shepherd, you never have to want spiritually. No matter what the world throws at you, you can be at peace. No fear overcomes those who follow the Shepherd as their King. He guides them through every trial, leading them faithfully into an eternity with Him.

Are you lacking contentment today? Look to the Shepherd for peace.

Watchful Love

*I have learned in whatever state I am,
to be content.*

PHILIPPIANS 4:11 NKJV

―――⟡⟡⟡―――

Paul wasn't writing about a grit-your-teeth
kind of contentment. He had learned to
trust deeply in God for all his needs, so the
apostle did not worry about future events. His
strength lay in God, who cared for his every
need, even when churches forgot him.
We, too, can be content in Jesus. If the boss
doesn't give us a raise or an unexpected bill
comes in, He knows it. Nothing escapes His
watchful love in our lives.

Contentment in Trouble

*The fear of the L*ORD *leads to life; then one rests content, untouched by trouble.*

PROVERBS 19:23

❧

God doesn't promise we will never suffer trouble, but He does promise something even more important. In the middle of trouble, we will experience real life— contentment in the middle of confusion, doubt, or turmoil. Which would you prefer, trouble and life in Jesus, or trouble on its own? You can't avoid trouble here on earth. But share life with Him, and contentment will follow.

Death

Eternal Perspective

"Where, O death, is your victory?
Where, O death, is your sting?"

1 CORINTHIANS 15:55

Nothing in this world ameliorates the pain of death. Losing one we love reaches deep into our souls. But with His sacrifice, Jesus permanently overcame the sting of mortality. Those who trust in Him do not live for a few short years, but for eternity. When sin takes their lives, they simply move into heaven. When we lose loved ones, our hearts feel pain. But if they gave their lives to Jesus, He is still victorious. In time, we will meet them again in paradise.

Our Hope

God raised him from the dead, freeing him from the agony of death, because it was impossible for death to keep its hold on him.

ACTS 2:24

———

Death could not grasp Jesus, the sinless One who died for the guilty. Though it clings to sinful beings, it had no claim on God's Son. Jesus is our only hope. Though sin deserves death, God's compassion made a way to free us from its agonies. When we give our poor, mortal lives to Jesus, we rise in Him, sharing His eternal life.

Death Will Die

The last enemy to be destroyed is death.

1 Corinthians 15:26

⚬⚬⚬

If Jesus conquered death, why do we still suffer with loved ones dying? Because today, we live in the promise of death's destruction, not its completion. God's Son has ransomed us through His sacrifice, but death still exists in our world. But one day, that will no longer be so. Jesus promises to destroy death entirely—death shall die, and heaven will be ours.

God's Promise

This is the promise that He has
promised us   eternal life.

1 JOHN 2:25 NKJV

The promise of eternal life comes straight
from God. Those who receive Jesus into their
hearts do not end their existence when they
stop breathing. Their last breath on earth
is merely a precursor of life in eternity with
Jesus. Today, you miss the one you lost, and
your heart aches. But in eternity, you will be
reunited and will share the joys of death conquered by the Savior. Until you meet again,
simply trust in His unfailing promise.

Doubt

The Only Way

"I am the way and the truth and the life. No one comes to the Father except through me."

JOHN 14:6

———※———

Plenty of people doubt Jesus. But those who have accepted Him as their Savior need not wallow in uncertainty. His Spirit speaks to ours, moment by moment, if we will only listen. He tells us God has shown us the way; we need not seek another path or truth. No other road leads to God. For a vibrant Christian life, we simply need to continue down the highway we're traveling with Jesus.

Be Faithful

*Good and upright is the LORD; therefore
he instructs sinners in his ways.*

PSALM 25:8

———

Don't know which way to turn or where
to go? God will show you. Just be faithful
to Him, and you will hear His still, small
voice guiding you; otherwise, circumstances and wise advisors will illuminate
the path you need to walk on.

Still doubting? Ask God for forgiveness
for sins that bar your communion with
Him. Soon, with a clean heart, you'll be
headed in the right direction.

Moving Mountains

"Whoever says to this mountain, 'Be removed and be cast into the sea,' and does not doubt. . .but believes. . .will have whatever he says."

MARK 11:23 NKJV

⸺◦⸺

Don't you wish you had faith like this? Christians often try to gear up to it, willing it with all their hearts. But that's not what God had in mind. Manipulating Him cannot work. Only when we fully trust in Him will He move our mountain—even if it's in an unexpected direction.

Compassion

Be merciful to those who doubt.

JUDE 1:22

If you've ever doubted (as we all have), you
can understand why this verse is in the
Bible. If well-meaning folks attacked you
for your uncertainty, it probably didn't
help—they just made you more nervous.
When questions enter our minds, we need
someone encouraging to come alongside us
and provide answers, not a critic who wants
to condemn our feelings. Knowing that, we
also need compassion for other doubters.
May we be the merciful ones who aid
those doubting hearts.

Eternity

Be Prepared

He has also set eternity in the hearts of men;
yet they cannot fathom what God has done
from beginning to end.

ECCLESIASTES 3:11

Though each of us has a bit of eternity in
our hearts, and we cannot rest unless we
know the Savior, we also cannot fathom
the works of God. That can either make us
dissatisfied and doubtful or relaxed, trusting
children who know their Father is in control
and will care for them from beginning to
end. Have you trusted Him who is the Alpha
and Omega? Are you prepared for eternity
with Him?

Always Secure

Your throne was established long ago;
you are from all eternity.

PSALM 93:2

❧

There was never a moment when God did
not exist. No scrap of time or eternity came
into being without Him, and nothing escapes
His powerful reign. That's good news for
His children. For whatever we face, now or
in our heavenly abode, we know our Father
is in control. No spiritual warfare or earthly
disaster lies beyond His plan. No wickedness
of Satan can take Him by surprise. Ours is the
eternal Lord, who has loved us from the start.
In Him, we are always secure.

Unchanging

Your word, O LORD, is eternal;
it stands firm in the heavens.

Psalm 119:89

———

The Word of God never changes. The
Father's commands do not alter, and neither does Jesus, the Word made flesh, or
His promise of salvation. Those who trust in
Him are secure as the Lord Himself, for He
does not change, and none of His promises
pass away unfulfilled. The eternal Lord and
all He commands stand firm. To gain eternity, simply receive Christ as your Savior;
then trust in Him.

Pure Delight

You have made known to me the path of life;
you will fill me with joy in your presence,
with eternal pleasures at your right hand.

PSALM 16:11

━━━

Rejoicing in God? Those who do not know Jesus cannot imagine it. You have to know Jesus to delight in His presence, just as you cannot enjoy a friend until you come to know each other and enjoy companionship. But knowing and loving God brings us, His children, joy in His presence and the prospect of undefined pleasures at His side. Are you prepared to share those joys with Jesus for eternity?

Source of Salvation

He became the source of eternal
salvation for all who obey him.

HEBREWS 5:9

⸺⸺

Salvation in Jesus is important to our earthly
lives. How many times has He dispelled
danger or helped us avoid it? How often
has sin failed to mar our lives because we
obeyed His commands? But Jesus is also the
source of salvation in eternity. Instead of
remaining forever in our earthly lives, God
planned to bring us into everlasting life with
Him, in His restored kingdom. In heaven,
we will praise His salvation, without end.

Faith
Loving Jesus

*Looking unto Jesus the author
and finisher of our faith.*

HEBREWS 12:2 KJV

God is writing a story of faith through
your life. What will it describe? Will it be
a chronicle of challenges overcome, like
the Old Testament story of Joseph? Or a
near tragedy turned into joy, like that of the
prodigal son? Whatever your account says,
if you love Jesus, the end is never in ques-
tion. Those who love Him finish in heaven,
despite their trials on earth. The long, weary
path ends in His arms. Today, write a chap-
ter in your faithful narrative of God's love.

He Never Fails

If we are faithless, he will remain faithful,
for he cannot disown himself.

2 TIMOTHY 2:13

⁓

Sometimes our faith fails, but Jesus never does. When we change for the worse, slip, or make a mistake, He is still the same faithful God He's always been. Though we may falter, He cannot. If we give in to the tempter's wiles, let us turn again to the faithful One. If we have trusted in Him, we can turn to Him for renewed forgiveness. His own faithfulness will not allow Him to deny us.

Perfection

His works are perfect, and all his ways are just.
A faithful God who does no wrong,
upright and just is he.

DEUTERONOMY 32:4

———

Many unbelievers, or even weakening believers living in crisis, complain that God is unfair. But Moses, who suffered much for God's people, knew better than that. God is always perfect, faithful, and just—it's rebellious humanity that lacks these qualities. We can have faith in God's perfection. He's never failed His people yet, though they have often been false. Trust in Him today. As He led His people to the Promised Land, He'll lead you home to Himself.

Spiritual Certainty

We live by faith, not by sight.

2 Corinthians 5:7

⸻

There is more than one way of seeing. We
view the world around us with our eyes, but
by doing so, we don't apprehend all there is
in life. Those things we "see" by faith cannot
be envisioned by our physical eyes. That's
why doubters disbelieve them. But when
God speaks to our hearts, it is as real as if
we'd viewed the truth plainly in front of us.
Like Paul, though our eyes cannot see it,
we have a spiritual certainty.

The Christian Life

Clearly no one is justified before God by the law, because, "The righteous will live by faith."

GALATIANS 3:11

———

Though some might claim it, crossing all your t's and dotting your i's spiritually does not make you a great Christian. Rules and regulations aren't what the Christian life is about—faith is. Obeying God and following Him as the Spirit leads challenges you to trust Him every moment of your life. With that kind of belief, you'll share His world-changing message.

Praise Him

Let them praise the name of the Lord,
for His name alone is exalted; His glory
is above the earth and heaven.

Psalm 148:13 nkjv

———

Trusting Jesus gives you a spectacular view of God's power. His work in your life increasingly opens your eyes to this glorious King who loves you. But those who do not know Him cannot praise Him. They are thoroughly blind to the glories of the One whom they have denied. Yet in the end, His glory will be apparent even to them. Whom do you follow—the glorious One or mere humans?

Our Hearts

Are you willing to recognize, you foolish fellow,
that faith without works is useless?

James 2:20 nasb

❦

Faith isn't faith if actions don't follow belief.
No matter what a person says, unless love,
compassion, and kindness accompany her
words, it would be foolish to consider
her Christian testimony believable.
Though works don't save us, they show
what's in our hearts. What are we
proving by our works today?

Family

Shine Brightly

Each one of you also must love his wife as he loves himself, and the wife must respect her husband.

EPHESIANS 5:33

—————

Marriage is a reciprocal relationship. For it to work well, both parties have to give and receive. If you share house space without the love and respect that make it a home, yours quickly becomes an empty existence. But that's not what God had in mind when He created marriage to reflect His own love for His people. He can help your marriage shine brightly for Him, if only you ask Him and are open to His will.

Building a House

The wise woman builds her house, but the foolish pulls it down with her hands.

PROVERBS 14:1 NKJV

—⋘⋙—

Did you know you can build a house? God says so. No, you won't use mortar, brick, and wood. But every Christian woman has the ability to build up her family with her wisdom, industry, and righteousness. Her faithful Christian character blesses those in her home. Today, are you building your house or tearing it down? Seek God, and He will help you make it strong.

Parents

*"Honor your father and your mother, that
your days may be long upon the land."*

EXODUS 20:12 NKJV

⸺◈⸺

When we honor our parents, we may not
spend much time in the Promised Land,
but God will bless us. Treating Mom and Dad
well improves our relationships with them
and gives our family security. As we treat our
children's grandparents well, we model the
actions of adult children, and our children
are more likely to treat us well, too.
Our Father God has special blessings for
those of us who respect our parents. Whether
it's Holy Land property or deeper love,
He gives us just what we need.

Appreciation for Mothers

Her children arise and call her blessed;
her husband also, and he praises her.

PROVERBS 31:28

⌘

Wouldn't every woman like to receive this
kind of praise? A few do. Yet though we
all need praise for a job well done, many
families forget to encourage their members.
When we have followed God faithfully, it
shows in our lives, but we still value others'
appreciation. Has a Christian mother been
a wonderful influence on your life? She'd
probably like to know that. Feel free to share
that praise with others, too.

Fear

Fear Will Flee

*Do not be afraid of sudden terror, nor of trouble
from the wicked when it comes; for the LORD
will be your confidence, and will keep your
foot from being caught.*

PROVERBS 3:25–26 NKJV

———

What do you have to fear, with God as your
confidence? He protects you from being
snared like a wild animal by the world's
troubles. With His hand over you, no sudden
event or evildoer's plot can destroy you. Give
Him your confidence, and fear will flee.

Fearing God

In the fear of the LORD there is strong confidence, and His children will have a place of refuge.

PROVERBS 14:26 NKJV

—✦—

There is only one right kind of fear—the fear of God. Not that we need to cower before Him, but we must respect and honor Him and His infinite power. Those who love Him also rightly fear Him. But those who fear God need fear nothing else. He is their refuge, the Protector whom nothing can bypass. Fear God, and you are safe.

Whom Do You Fear?

"I tell you, my friends, do not be afraid of those who kill the body and after that can do no more."

LUKE 12:4

Whom do you fear? If it's anyone other than God, take heart. You need not concern yourself with anything that person can do to you. Even those who can take your life can't change your eternal destination. So if someone doesn't like your faith, don't sweat it. Put your trust in God and serve Him faithfully, and you need not fear.

Freedom from Fear

You came near when I called you,
and you said, "Do not fear."

LAMENTATIONS 3:57

———

As tentacles of fear attempt to wrap themselves about us, we struggle to escape. But
freedom lies in our Redeemer. His still,
small voice speaks to our hearts: "Do not
fear. What terror is greater than I?"
He who created the universe will never be
taken unaware by troubles or disturbed by
our dread. They cannot disrupt His plan.
The future lies clear before His eyes,
and He saves us from every harm.

Secure in the Father

*For you did not receive a spirit that makes you a
slave again to fear, but you received the Spirit of
sonship. And by him we cry, "Abba, Father."*

ROMANS 8:15

As part of God's family, you need never dread
anything. He who rules the universe adopted
you. Since your loving Father no longer con-
demns you for sin, panic need not rule your
life. Fear no retribution, because your elder
brother Jesus shed His blood for you, cover-
ing every sin. God's child always remains
secure in her Abba, "Daddy."

Forgiveness

Blessing of Forgiveness

*[Our] sins have been forgiven
on account of his name.*

1 John 2:12

Who could do something wonderful
enough to earn God's forgiveness? No human work can buy it. God forgives because
of who He is, not because of who we are
or what we do. That's encouraging, because we can't earn forgiveness by our own
perfection. Instead, forgiveness becomes
the great blessing of our Christian life that
makes living for Jesus possible. We obey
God to show our appreciation, not to
gain entry into His kingdom.

An End to Mourning

"Blessed are those who mourn,
for they will be comforted."

MATTHEW 5:4

How often do we think of mourning as a
good thing? But when it comes to sin, it is.
Those who sorrow over their own sinfulness will turn to God for forgiveness. When
He willingly responds to their repentance,
mourning ends. Comforted by God's pardon, transformed sinners celebrate—and
joyous love for Jesus replaces sorrow.

The Price of Forgiveness

And according to the law almost all things are
purified with blood, and without shedding
of blood there is no remission.

Hebrews 9:22 NKJV

Many people in our world would like cheap
forgiveness. They want someone to say
they are okay, but they don't want to pay
any price for their wrongdoing. That's not
what the scriptures say. Remission of sins
comes at a high price—sacrificial blood, the
blood of Jesus. Jesus says you are worth this
expense, and you are clean in Him. Put sin
away and rejoice in His deep love for you.

Pass It On

"If you forgive others for their transgressions, your heavenly Father will also forgive you."

MATTHEW 6:14, NASB

Forgiveness isn't only something God gives us. He designed it to be passed on to others. Doing that, we learn the value of the pardon the Father offered us. Even when everything in us screams, "No, I can't forgive," He empowers us to do so, if we trust in Him. Our loving Father never commands us to actions He cannot also strengthen us to do.

Friendship

Chosen Family

There is a friend that sticketh closer than a brother.

PROVERBS 18:24 KJV

Family relationships range from the wonderful to the disturbing, and we get whatever God gives us. But we choose our friends based on common interests and experiences. Often this "chosen family" seems closer to us than siblings. Yet neither clings closer than our elder brother Jesus. He teaches us how to love blood relatives and those we choose. No matter whether or not we're related, when we love in Him, that love sticks fast.

Disconnect from the World

*Whosoever therefore will be a friend
of the world is the enemy of God.*

JAMES 4:4 KJV

There are good friendships and bad ones.
When Christ becomes your best friend, other
relationships may become distant. Old,
carnal friendships no longer seem so attrac-
tive. Your lifestyles clash, and old friends
become confused. But this separation is part
of God's plan of holiness. Jesus disconnects
you from the world and draws you close to
His people—Christian friends who share your
love for Him. Together, you may reach out to
those old friends for Jesus, too.

Importance of Friendship

Do not forsake your friend and the friend of your father, and do not go to your brother's house when disaster strikes you—better a neighbor nearby than a brother far away.

PROVERBS 27:10

Friendship is important to God, or He would not encourage us to hold fast to it. As Christians, we've known times when other believers seemed closer than our kin. God has brought us into a new family—His own—where faith becomes more important than blood. Through Him, our love expands, and we help each other when trouble strikes. No matter where you go, God's people are near.

Our Best Friend

A righteous man is cautious in friendship,
but the way of the wicked leads them astray.

PROVERBS 12:26

———

We need friends. But there are those who
will lead us into trouble and those who will
encourage us and lift us up in our faith,
drawing us ever nearer to God. Before we
draw near to others, do we consider their
spiritual impact on us? If God is our best
friend, let us be cautious not to be led astray.
When we share friendship with Jesus and
our earthly friends, we are truly blessed.

Giving

Prayerful Giving

Give, and it shall be given unto you; good measure, pressed down. . .and running over.

LUKE 6:38 KJV

———

Need an example of how to give? Look to God. To those who give generously, He gives overflowing, abundant blessings. In this fallen world, we need to be careful to whom we give support. Dishonest people or those who oppose God should not be our charitable choices. But many Christian ministries do good work and need our support. Faithful churches need our giving. As we donate prayerfully, God will bless us in return.

Want vs. Need

"Give us this day our daily bread."

MATTHEW 6:11 NKJV

⊰⊱

Jesus tells us here to ask God for our daily
needs, and we may do that frequently. Let's
remember that even the smallest things,
such as the bread we put on the table, come
from God. Yet, have we forgotten that all our
food comes from our heavenly Father? God
forgets nothing we need. So if we don't have
steak instead of hamburgers, could it be
because we want, but don't need, it?

Share His Love

"It is more blessed to give than to receive."

ACTS 20:35

※

Christmas has become a time of receiving—
to the point where greed motivates more
people than blessing. But Paul reminds us
that getting what we want is not the greatest
blessing. We know that when we see the
delight in a child's eyes at receiving a longed-
for item. Our heavenly Father loves to see
the same joy in our eyes, when He helps us
in less tangible ways. That's why He tells us
to share His love with others.

Getting What You Give

Whoever sows sparingly will also reap sparingly, and whoever sows generously will also reap generously.

2 CORINTHIANS 9:6

⚬⚬⚬

What you give is what you get. That's true in life, and it's also true spiritually. Anyone who tries to hold their finances close will be letting go of spiritual blessings, while the person who shares generously gains in so many ways. It's hard to give up worldly treasures, but when you give in the name of Jesus, you will never run short.

God as Father

Loving Correction

For whom the LORD loves He corrects, just as a father the son in whom he delights.

PROVERBS 3:12 NKJV

———∞∞∞———

Do you feel the pain of God's correction? Take heart, since it shows He loves you. Just as a loving father will not let his child walk in a dangerous place, your heavenly Father is redirecting you onto another path. Today's discipline may hurt, but in days to come, your sorrow will turn to joy as you reap the blessing that follows obedience. Your Father loves you deeply.

Compassion

A father to the fatherless, a defender of widows,
is God in his holy dwelling.

PSALM 68:5

————

God's love is very tender toward those who
hurt. Children who have lost their fathers
and women who have lost their husbands
can count on His compassion. When we
lose a loved one, do we focus on the Father's
gentleness? We are more likely to complain
that He did not extend life than to praise
Him for His care. But when we feel the most
pain, we also receive the largest portion of
God's comfort. What hurts His children
hurts Him, too.

Heavenly Father

The mighty God, The everlasting Father.

ISAIAH 9:6 KJV

If you have accepted Jesus as your Savior, God is always your Father. Distance, disagreement, or death cannot change that, though each may separate you from your earthly father. But a human parent is neither mighty nor everlasting and may fail physically or spiritually. Only your heavenly Father will always be there for you, guiding you every step of the way. When you need help, call on your Father; He will never fail.

Children of God

*Because you are sons, God sent the Spirit of
his Son into our hearts, the Spirit who calls out,
"Abba, Father."*

GALATIANS 4:6

God draws His children near, connecting
them firmly to Himself through the Son
and the Holy Spirit. There is no division in
the Godhead when it comes to loving God's
adopted children. With the Spirit, we call out,
"Abba, Daddy," to the Holy One who loved
us enough to call us to Himself, despite our
sin. Through Jesus' sacrifice and the Spirit's
work, God the Father cleanses us and opens
communications, so we can follow Him truly.

He Loves You This Much!

How great is the love the Father has lavished on us, that we should be called children of God! And that is what we are!

1 JOHN 3:1

———

God does not give His love in dribs and drabs. He lavishes it on us when we come to Him in faith. All along, He was waiting to make us His children, and we were the ones who resisted. But once we face Him as His children, God's love lets loose in our lives. Nothing is too good for His obedient children. Praise God that He loves you that much!

Turn to Him

*"I will be a Father to you, and you shall be My sons
and daughters, says the Lord Almighty."*

2 Corinthians 6:18 nkjv

Only unconfessed sin can separate you from

the Father. But God never desires such

distance. He wants to draw near, like a lov-

ing Father who holds His child, provides for

her, and helps her at every turn.

Though your earthly father was less than

perfect, your heavenly Father is not. He

heals your hurts, solves your problems, and

offers His love at every turn. All you need

to do is turn to Him in love.

God as Refuge

Stand Firm

The LORD has become my fortress, and my God the rock in whom I take refuge.

PSALM 94:22

Are you under attack by friends, family, or coworkers? If it comes because of your obedience to the Lord, stand firm in the face of their comments. He will defend you. If you face harsh words or nasty attitudes, remain kind, and He will assist you. Should your boss do you wrong, don't worry. Those who are against a faithful Christian are also against Him, and God will somehow make things right.

Our Refuge

The LORD Almighty is the one you are to regard
as holy. . .and he will be a sanctuary.

ISAIAH 8:13–14

—◆◆◆—

When you live in awe of God—when He alone

is Lord of your life—you have nothing to

fear. If fears or enemies assail you, a place

of refuge is always nearby. God never throws

His children to the wolves. Instead, He

protects them in His holy place. With Jesus

as your Savior, you always have a

peaceful place to go to.

Receive His Strength

The LORD also will be a refuge for the oppressed,
a refuge in times of trouble.

PSALM 9:9 NKJV

The Psalms often speak of God as a refuge.
Whether you face something large, like
oppression, or something much smaller,
He wants you to turn to Him in troublous
times. Size does not matter, but your trust
in Jesus does. Nothing you face is a shock
to Him—He knows your troubles and has
not deserted you. So go to your refuge and
take strength from Him.

Nothing Is Hidden

Nothing in all creation is hidden from God's sight.

HEBREWS 4:13

———

Good or bad, nothing escapes God's notice. None of it is unknown to the Creator of the universe. And because He knows all, we can completely trust in God. He protects us from the wicked and supports the good in our lives, because He knows just how both will touch us. When sorrow or trouble comes our way, we can count on His using it to benefit us—here and in eternity.

God's Faithfulness

Always Faithful

I will never leave thee, nor forsake thee.

Hebrews 13:5 KJV

Even when fear or stress challenges you, you
need never deal with it single-handedly, if
Jesus rules your life. When your life seems in
shambles around you, He offers strength and
comfort for a hurting heart. God never gives
up on you. His love cannot change. Today,
delight in the One who never deserts you.

Nothing Is Impossible

"For nothing is impossible with God."

LUKE 1:37

⸻

The angel spoke these words to Mary as he gave her the news that the aged Elizabeth would bear a child. God deals with the impossible in our lives, too. We do not bear a Savior, but how has He helped us understand impossible relationships, juggle a hectic schedule, or help a hurting friend? God offers aid, whatever we face. Nothing is impossible for the One at work in our lives. What impossibilities can He deal with in your life? Have you trusted Him for help?

He Is Faithful

Blessed is he whose help is the God of Jacob. . .
the LORD, who remains faithful forever.

PSALM 146:5–6

————

You are not the only one who has experienced God's faithfulness. Through the years, believers have experienced His provision. Read Old Testament accounts of those who have never seen Him fail. Watch His acts in the New Testament as He showed the church that it could trust Him. God cannot fail His children, and He will not fail you. Trust in the God of Jacob, and pass on your testimony of His faithfulness.

God Offers Hope

"For I know the plans I have for you," declares the
LORD, *"plans to prosper you and not to harm you,
plans to give you hope and a future."*

JEREMIAH 29:11

❧

As Judah headed into exile, conquered by
a savage pagan people, God offered them
hope. He still had a good plan for them, one
that would come out of suffering. Their
prosperity was not at an end, though their
path through hardship had begun.
When God leads you up a rocky path, your
hope and future remain secure in Him.
Faithful trust is all He asks of you.

God's Help

Call on Him

Our help is in the name of the LORD,
the Maker of heaven and earth.

PSALM 124:8

The name God told to Moses, "I AM WHO I AM," describes His unchanging nature. So here, when the Unchanging One promises to help us, that assurance never alters. What in heaven or on earth could be too powerful or too much trouble for its Maker? Nothing is greater than God, not even our biggest challenge. We need only call His name.

All-Powerful

*God is our refuge and strength, an
ever-present help in trouble.*

PSALM 46:1

—◦◦◦—

When we face serious troubles, people often
cannot provide the solution. Limited by
human frailty, even the most generous of
them can only help us so much. In every
trouble, we have a greater asset, if we believe
in Jesus. Our all-powerful Creator offers
protection from harm and strength for the
longest trial. He always wants to come to our
aid. Facing a trouble of any size?
Turn to Him today.

Never Forgotten

Who is like the LORD our God. . .who stoops
down to look on the heavens and the earth?

PSALM 113:5–6

———

This all-powerful Lord, to whom the
heavens and earth are small, cares not
just for your universe, but for you. The
verses that follow these describe His love
for even the most humble person. Though
you may face times of struggle, your awesome Lord will never forget you. One day,
as verse 8 of this psalm promises, even
the humble can sit with princes.

Ask for Help

Let us then approach the throne of grace with confidence, so that we may receive mercy and find grace to help us in our time of need.

HEBREWS 4:16

Don't feel shy about approaching Jesus with all your cares. As God's child, you have a special place in His heart. When you have failed, you need not fear coming to the King of kings for mercy and grace. He is just waiting for you to admit the problem and ask for help. Seek Jesus' aid, whatever your trouble. That's what He wants you to do.

Purposeful Plan

And we know that all things work together for good to those who love God, to those who are the called according to His purpose.

ROMANS 8:28 NKJV

Life doesn't always look ideal to us. When finances are tight, family problems are serious, or things just don't seem to go our way, we may doubt that God is working in our lives. That's the time we need to reread this verse and take heart. Even things that don't seem good have a purpose in God's plan. As Christians, we can trust in Him, even when life is less than perfect.

God's Love

Open Door

"For God so loved the world that he gave his one and only Son, that whoever believes in him shall not perish but have eternal life."

JOHN 3:16

———

These words are God's open door to those who believe in His Son. The barrier between God's holiness and man's sinfulness disintegrates when we believe in Jesus' sacrifice for human sin. But we must walk through that open door, with faith, to inherit the eternal life God offers. Have you taken that step, or are you still outside the door?

Tender Love

This is love: not that we loved God, but that he loved us and sent his Son as an atoning sacrifice for our sins.

1 JOHN 4:10

We weren't sitting around thinking about loving God before He touched our lives. God began the process before we were even born. He sent His Son to bring us into communion with Him, and His Spirit drew us into a relationship with Him. We respond to God's overwhelmingly tender love when we invite Jesus into our lives. Even so, many years of obedience show our gratitude, but they never repay His loving compassion.

Gift of Love

The LORD takes delight in his people.

PSALM 149:4

———

God doesn't just like you—He delights in you. You are so special to Him; He brought you into His salvation so He could spend eternity with you. God loves each of His children in a special way. You aren't just another in a long line of His people. He knows every bit of you, your faithfulness and failures, and loves each part of you "to pieces." We could never earn such love— it is His special gift to each of us. Let's rejoice in that blessing today.

God's Love Is at Work

*We have known and believed the love that God has
for us. God is love, and he who abides in
love abides in God, and God in him.*

1 John 4:16 NKJV

———

Trusting in Jesus, you have felt God's love
at work in your inner being. The vibrant
connection that only Christians experience
becomes the center of your life. If you are
faithful, His eternal life renews you from
head to toe and shines forth vibrantly. Your
Spirit-inspired words and actions truly
portray God's love to the world.

By Your Side

Love is patient, love is kind. It does not envy,
it does not boast, it is not proud.

1 CORINTHIANS 13:4

———

God's love is not short-tempered or short-lived. Unlike human love, it never gives up on you, even on those long, discouraging days when your job is a strain, family life becomes confused, and you hardly know where to turn. In such stressful times, your heavenly Father puts up with all of it, right beside you. He's not out there somewhere—He's close by your side.

God's Mercy

Appreciation for Mercy

The LORD your God is a merciful God;
he will not abandon or destroy you.

DEUTERONOMY 4:31

❦

Even when we fail God, He does not fail
us. He knows our frailty and has mercy
when we come to Him seeking forgiveness and wanting to change our ways.
Mercy never holds grudges or seeks
revenge, but it wants the best for forgiven
sinners. So our merciful Lord calls us to
make changes that show we appreciate
what He has done for us. Is some
appreciation called for in your life?

Endurance

As you know, we consider blessed those who have perseverance. You have heard of Job's perseverance and have seen what the Lord finally brought about. The Lord is full of compassion and mercy.

JAMES 5:11

Endurance in faith, hard as it may seem, brings happiness. Trials are not a sign of God's disfavor or His will to carelessly punish His children. The tenderhearted Savior never acts cruelly. But through troubles, we draw close to Him and see God's power at work in our lives. Then, like Job, when we persevere in faith, God rewards us bountifully.

Mercy Triumphs

Mercy triumphs over judgment!

JAMES 2:13

━━◆◆◆━━

Not only is God merciful to us, He expects us to pass that blessing on to others. Instead of becoming the rule enforcers in this world, He wants us to paint a picture of the tender love He has for fallen people and to call many other sinners into His love. When we criticize the world and do not show compassion, we lose the powerful witness we were meant to have. As you stand firm for Jesus, may mercy also triumph in your life.

Rebirth and Renewal

He saved us, not because of righteous things we
had done, but because of his mercy. He saved
us through the washing of rebirth and
renewal by the Holy Spirit.

TITUS 3:5

Could we save ourselves? No way! Even our
best efforts fall far short of God's perfection. If God had left us on our own, we'd be
eternally separated from Him. But graciously,
the Father reached down to us through His
Son, sacrificing Jesus on the cross. Then
the Spirit touched our lives in rebirth and
renewal. Together, the three Persons of the
Godhead saved us in merciful love.

Joy in Our Troubles

Great is your love, reaching to the heavens;
your faithfulness reaches to the skies.

PSALM 57:10

———

Has God's mercy touched your life so
deeply that you wanted to shout His
praises to the skies? That's how the
psalmist felt as he trusted in God,
despite his troubles. When we look to
God in our troubles, our burdened hearts
can still find joy. Though we are small and
weak, He is most powerful. His strength
will overcome our deepest problems,
if only we let it.

Overflowing Mercy

O Israel, put your hope in the LORD, for with
the LORD is unfailing love and with him
is full redemption.

PSALM 130:7

⸻

Why hope in God, even in dire situations?
Because every one of His people greatly
needs His overflowing mercy. Our lives
are frail, but He is not. Jesus brings the
redemption we require. No matter what we
face, Jesus walks with us. We need only trust
faithfully that His salvation is on the way.

God's Provision

God Meets Our Needs

"He has brought down rulers from their thrones but has lifted up the humble. He has filled the hungry with good things but has sent the rich away empty."

LUKE 1:52–53

God provides for every one of His children, even the most humble. Wealth cannot gain His favor nor poverty destroy it. The Father does not look at the pocketbook, but at the heart. Those who love Him, though they may lack cash, see their needs fulfilled, but unbelievers who own overflowing store-houses harvest empty hearts. God never ignores His children's needs. What has He given you today?

He Will Never Fail

You open your hand and satisfy the
desires of every living thing.

PSALM 145:16

———

Our faithful Lord provides for all His
created beings. Will He fail to care for you?
How could He satisfy the needs of the smallest birds and beasts, yet forget His human
child? God is always faithful. Though we fail,
He will not. He cannot forget His promises
of love and will never forget to provide for
your every need.

His Gifts

*If, by the trespass of the one man, death reigned
through that one man, how much more will
those who receive God's abundant provision of
grace and of the gift of righteousness reign in
life through the one man, Jesus Christ.*

ROMANS 5:17

———

What greater gift could God give us than

His grace? Once, death ruled over us.

Now, life in Christ commands our days.

As we ponder God's compassion, do we

appreciate Christ's sacrifice? Any spiri-

tual value we have comes from His gifts.

We can never repay Him, but are we living

to show how much we care?

Trust God

*Abraham answered, "God himself will provide
the lamb for the burnt offering, my son."*

GENESIS 22:8

—◆—

Though God had commanded Abraham to
sacrifice his son Isaac, the patriarch had
faith his son would not die. All it took was a
ram, caught in a bush. Because of Abraham's
faith, the sheep was just where he needed it
at the right moment. God provided just what
was necessary—a sacrifice and a living son.
Do you need God's provision today? Trust
the God who made a way for Abraham to
make a way for you, too.

Let His Light Shine

For Christ's sake, I delight in weaknesses, in
insults, in hardships, in persecutions, in
difficulties. For when I am weak, then I am strong.

2 Corinthians 12:10

⸻

Only God can make you strong in the
weak places. In those spots of persecution
and hardship, His power and grace shine
through your fragile vessel as you live as a
faithful Christian. When you feel broken
and useless, trust in Him to fill your flaws,
and His light will shine through the cracks
of your pain and reach a hurting world.

God's Word

The Living Word

The word of God is living and active and sharper than any two-edged sword, and piercing as far as the division of soul and spirit.

HEBREWS 4:12 NASB

The Bible is not a dead book. The writer of Hebrews says it lives, and those who trust in Jesus can attest to this truth. Have you read a scripture and felt God knew just what you required, because it related to your needs in a special way? Then you've experienced the living Word of God that pierces your soul and spirit. Live by it, in His love.

Knowing God

In the beginning was the Word, and the Word
was with God, and the Word was God.

JOHN 1:1

―――

Want a picture of God's Word? Look at
Jesus, the embodiment of everything the
Father wanted to say to us. You can't do that
if you don't read the Book that tells of Him.
Maybe that's why God takes it personally
when we decide not to read His Word.
We're ignoring His tender commands and
pushing aside His love. God's scriptures
communicate with His children. How can
we know Him without His Word?

Flawless Words

Every word of God is flawless.

PROVERBS 30:5

⸻

Maybe you've had days when you've been
tempted to doubt this verse. You wanted to
go in one direction, and God's Word said
to go in another. But if you were wise, you
trusted in its truth instead of following your
own way. After all, can you claim that your
every word is error free? No. How much
better to follow in the perfect way of your
Lord, who willingly shares His wisdom. To
avoid many of the faults of this world,
trust the flawless Word of God.

Commitment and Action

Now by this we know that we know Him,
if we keep His commandments.

1 JOHN 2:3 NKJV

———

How do you know you are a Christian? By the
way you follow your Lord's commandments.
Salvation is not just a matter of feeling His
touch in your life. Faith is not simply a
matter of emotion; it requires commitment
and action, too. Real love for God contains
a passion for following Him. Love Him, and
your life serves Him, too.

Living Consistently

*Then Jesus said to those Jews who believed Him,
"If you abide in My word, you are My
disciples indeed."*

JOHN 8:31 NKJV

———∞———

Here, Jesus talks to His disciples about a
habitual lifestyle. He wanted them to live
consistently in the truth He had taught
them, not pull His Word out once a week or
live by it once in a while. But this verse isn't
only for those who walked with Jesus during
His earthly ministry. Today, His Spirit helps
us live consistently for Him. As we connect
with the scriptures and obey His commands,
we become disciples, too.

Guidance

Safe in His Will

*Your hand will guide me, your right
hand will hold me fast.*

PSALM 139:10

Need to make a life changing decision?
God wants to be part of it. As the psalmist
understood, allowing Him to guide your
steps means you won't get off track and
land in a nasty situation. For the believer,
the best place to be is in the palm of God's
hand, safe from harm and in the center
of His will.

Every Step of the Way

He will be our guide even to the end.

PSALM 48:14

———

When we are facing dire troubles, God never deserts us. As life ebbs away, He does not step back from our need. No, the Eternal One guides us every step of the way, whether life is joyous or discouraging. God never gives up on you and never fails you. So don't give up on yourself. When times are hard, grab onto Him more firmly. He will never leave you nor forsake you. And in the end, you will step into His arms in heaven.

You Can't Go Wrong

*"In your unfailing love you will lead the people you
have redeemed. In your strength you will guide
them to your holy dwelling."*

EXODUS 15:13

By following Jesus, you always head in the
right direction. Though the way may seem
dark or convoluted, and you may often wonder if you're on the right track, as His Spirit
leads you, you cannot go wrong. Your powerful Lord directs you in His everlasting way.
If you start to go wrong, He will guide your
steps. God's love never deserts His
obedient child.

The Light

When Jesus spoke again to the people, he said, "I am the light of the world. Whoever follows me will never walk in darkness, but will have the light of life."

John 8:12

————— ❧ —————

Following the light of the world means you can see where you're headed. Even when life becomes confusing and totally dark, your goal hasn't changed, and you keep heading in the right direction. Walking in Jesus' light, though you hit a dark patch, you remain on the road with the Savior, and in Him you always see enough to take the next step.

Hope

Hope in Him

*Put your hope in God, for I will yet praise him,
my Savior and my God.*

PSALM 42:5–6

———

Where else should the believer place her hope? No human has power to turn her life around without Jesus. No solution lies beyond Him, and He never pushes her away. When the world becomes harsh, she still receives His gentle encouragement. Though you wait long, and the path seems hard, hold on to Jesus. Words of praise will pass your lips as you see His salvation accomplished. Your God will never let you fall.

Overflow with Hope

May the God of hope fill you with all joy and peace as you trust in him, so that you may overflow with hope by the power of the Holy Spirit.

ROMANS 15:13

———

Where does hope come from? From God. Unbelievers may have moments of wishful thinking or snatches of optimism in their lives, but they cannot exist in an abiding hope. Christians, filled with the Spirit, see hope overflow as they live in Christ, fulfilling the will of the Father. Have faith? Then you have every reason to hope each day.

Be Strong

Be strong and take heart,
all you who hope in the LORD.

PSALM 31:24

※

Hope is not some weak, airy-fairy kind of thing. It takes strength to put your trust in God when life batters your heart and soul. Weaklings rarely hold on to positive expectation for long, because it takes too much from them. But the spiritually strong put their trust in God and let Him lift up their hearts in hope. Then battering may come, but it cannot destroy them. Hope makes Christians stronger still.

Unfailing Love

The LORD delights in those who. . .
put their hope in his unfailing love.

PSALM 147:11

━━◦◦◦◦━━

We can hope in a lot of things that fail us
miserably, or we can enjoy a blind optimism
that leads us into trouble. But when we hope
in God, who has loved us completely, our
faith cannot fail. Could the One who delights
in our trust forget to bless our anticipation
of an eternity with Him?
Make God joyful today as you put your
trust in His everlasting love.

120

Prosperity Returns

"Then I will make up to you for the years that the swarming locust has eaten."

JOEL 2:25 NASB

———

Those of us who rejoice in God can trust that even though the consuming locusts of life destroy our blessings, God will replace them. Though hardship makes us struggle awhile, God turns the situation around and pours out blessings on His faithful people. Prosperity returns to those who love Him well, if we determinedly love Him. In heaven or on earth, the blessing appears again.

Where Is Your Hope?

*Find rest, O my soul, in God alone;
my hope comes from him.*

PSALM 62:5

——

Those who hope in worldly things are
destined for frustration and disappointment,
but Christians rest in God, so instead of
frustration, they receive blessing and
confidence from their powerful Savior.
Where is your hope today? If it's in things,
you are bound to worry, but hope in God is
always fulfilled. Relax in the knowledge that
He never fails.

Joy

Obedience = Joy

*"I have told you this so that my joy may be in
you and that your joy may be complete."*

JOHN 15:11

What wouldn't we do to share Jesus' complete joy! But this verse comes after one of
Jesus' commands to obedience. Ah, now do
we change our minds? Does joy suddenly
become impossible? When Jesus calls us
to act, do we follow, or do we decide it's too
hard and give up immediately? Let's keep
our eyes on the outcome—the joy of our Lord
filling our lives. Then obedience, too, may
become a joy.

Joy Will Come

My lips will shout for joy when I sing praise to you—I, whom you have redeemed.

PSALM 71:23

⟨⟩

Having trouble finding joy in your life today? Do what the psalmists often did and remind yourself what God has already done for you. How many ways has following Him blessed you? Begin by thanking Him for His saving grace, and the joy starts, no matter what you face today. Your lips will show the delight in your heart.

Sorrow to Joy

"I will turn their mourning into gladness;
I will give them comfort and joy
instead of sorrow."

JEREMIAH 31:13

❦

In the midst of Israel's sorrow at its captivity by a pagan people, God promised a time of joy, when they would return to their land and be His people again. Are you separated from joy right now? Perhaps sin has overtaken your life, and you long to again lean close to God and share His tender love. Ask Him to turn your heart away from this barren landscape and return it to Him. Your sorrow can turn to joy.

The Kingdom of Heaven

*Sorrowful, yet always rejoicing; poor,
yet making many rich; having nothing,
and yet possessing everything.*

2 CORINTHIANS 6:10

⚬⚬⚬

What a description of a Christian! Rejoicing in sorrow seems rather contradictory, doesn't it? How could the apostle Paul feel joy in such circumstances? Because God works in even less-than-perfect situations. In fact, He often works most powerfully when troubles load our plate. What do we have to rejoice in? The wonderful work God does in our lives, no matter what we face. We always possess the kingdom of heaven.

Praise God—No Matter What

The king will rejoice in God; all who
swear by God's name will praise him.

PSALM 63:11

———

Need some joy in your life? Start praising

God, and no matter what messy situations

you face today, you'll begin rejoicing. Praise

Him for who He is—His immense, loving

nature that has blessed you so much. Thank

Him for the love He's showered on you. As

you remember His love, sorrow loses its

grasp on your life.

Knowing God

Close to Jesus

Be still, and know that I am God.

PSALM 46:10

———❧———

So often, we seek to do things for God or to
prove our Christian witness. But if we become simply caught up in busyness, we lose
the distinction of our faith: a close relationship with Jesus. Knowing God is not about
what we do, but whom we love. Our good
works mean little if we disconnect from
Him. Spend time being still with God today,
and a deepened knowledge of Him will
be your blessing.

God Is Great

I know that the LORD is great, that our Lord is greater than all gods.

PSALM 135:5

❦

Other "gods" contend with Jesus in the marketplace of ideas, and devout Christians may encounter contention. But just as the psalmist recognized God's greatness, we can, too, as we look at the world around us. No other would-be deity shows forth its glory in creation. No other has provided His gracious salvation. If our Lord controls our lives, how can we look to any other gods?

Know Him Intimately

"I will take you as my own people, and I will be your God. Then you will know that I am the LORD your God, who brought you out from under the yoke of the Egyptians."

EXODUS 6:7

—❧—

God freed the Hebrews from slavery and brought them to their new land. But He didn't stop there. Today, He still proves Himself to people by freeing them from sin's slavery and creating loving relationships with them. Has God freed you from sin? Then know Him intimately. Draw near and enjoy His blessings, no matter what "slavery" you've faced before.

Father and Son

We know also that the Son of God has come and has given us understanding, so that we may know him who is true. And we are in him who is true even in his Son Jesus Christ. He is the true God and eternal life.

1 JOHN 5:20

⸺⸺⸺

How do we know God? Through His Son,
Jesus, who helps us understand the love of
His Father. There is no space, no difference
of opinion, between Father and Son. When
we know the Son, we know God truly.
Trust in one is trust in both.

Live Devotedly

*Do you not know that you are the temple of God
and that the Spirit of God dwells in you?*

1 CORINTHIANS 3:16 NKJV

God lives within you, not in a distant place.
When you act according to His Word, He
acts. When you fail, people may begin to
doubt Him. That's why Paul encourages you
to live devotedly for your Lord. As one of His
people, you're filled with His potent Spirit,
who empowers you to live a holy life.
Live in His strength always.

Loving God

Perfecting Our Love

Jesus replied: " 'Love the Lord your God with all your heart and with all your soul and with all your mind.' "

MATTHEW 22:37

———

This simple command can be a real challenge, can't it? No matter how we try, in our own power, to love God completely, we always seem to fail somewhere. Only as God's Spirit works in our hearts will our whole being become ever more faithful. God works in us day by day, perfecting our love. Ask Him to help you love Him today.

Love Is Action

Dear friends, let us love one another, for love comes from God. Everyone who loves has been born of God and knows God.

1 JOHN 4:7

———

Want to see love? Look at God. Seeking love in this world is bound to be confusing. But in our Lord, we see the clean, clear lines of real love—love we can share with our families, friends, and fellow believers. Love for our enemies. Love for our Savior. Apart from God, we cannot truly and sacrificially love others. Love isn't just a feeling, but the actions we take as we follow Him.

Seeing God

No one has seen God at any time. If we love
one another, God abides in us, and His
love has been perfected in us.

1 JOHN 4:12 NKJV

⚬⚬⚬

How do we see God? Often, it's through other
people. That's why it's important to have a
compassionate Christian witness—people
see you and think God is like you, if you
claim His name. In that way, many people
have gotten erroneous concepts about the
Savior. But many more have come to love
Him through faithful testimonies. Today,
you can love others and show them clearly
what Jesus looks like.

Gentle Reminder

If a man say, I love God, and hateth his brother,
he is a liar: for he that loveth not his brother
whom he hath seen, how can he love God
whom he hath not seen?

1 JOHN 4:20 KJV

John's letter surely knows how to challenge
us. Now we wonder, *Do I love God at all?*
Surely, on our own, we couldn't. But when
we accept God and receive His love, our
attitude changes. In Jesus, we can love even
a bothersome brother. Sometimes, we just
need a gentle reminder.

Sweet Sacrifice

*Live a life of love, just as Christ loved us
and gave himself up for us as a fragrant
offering and sacrifice to God.*

EPHESIANS 5:2

—

We don't think of sacrifice as being sweet.
More often, we see it as hardship or
drudgery. But when we have experienced
the delightfulness of Jesus' sacrifice,
which brought us into a love relationship
with Him, we understand just what this
verse means. Yet, God calls us not only
to receive love but to pass it on to others
who also need to understand the
sweetness of His sacrifice.

Learn from Jesus

"A new command I give you: Love one another.
As I have loved you, so you must love one another."

JOHN 13:34

———

How do we know how to love? We learn from
Jesus. The Master had been with His disciples for three years when He spoke these
words, and they had seen His love in action.
We see it, too, in God's Word and in the lives
of faithful believers. In His power, we can
take what we know and follow Jesus, living
out the words He spoke and the good
examples we have seen.

138

New Life

Looks Can Be Deceiving

*Therefore we do not lose heart. Though outwardly
we are wasting away, yet inwardly we are
being renewed day by day.*

2 CORINTHIANS 4:16

On the outside, people see us getting older
and frailer. But looks are deceiving. As
Christians, we constantly build our belief,
if we walk consistently with God. We're
growing deeper in faith, being spiritually
renewed every day. God's glory lies ahead
of us, as on earth we learn to appreciate His
love and compassion. Undaunted, we look
ahead to eternity and a new body, made
perfect by our Savior.

Life-Altering Impact

We were therefore buried with him through baptism into death in order that, just as Christ was raised from the dead through the glory of the Father, we too may live a new life.

ROMANS 6:4

⬦⬦⬦

Baptism is a picture of the old, sinful nature's death and the new faith-life God gives those who trust in Him. Belief in Jesus has a life-altering impact. One moment, a sinful person is dead, held in sin's grasp. The next, she becomes an entirely new person, alive in her Savior. Only Jesus offers this glorious freedom. Has He given it to you?

Living in the Light

*In him was life, and that life
was the light of men.*

JOHN 1:4

———✦———

Jesus is a Christian's life and light, as
anyone who has walked with Him for a
while can tell you. Everything is different
once He enters a soul. As a result, the new
believer begins to make changes, clean-
ing out the dark corners of her existence
so that the bright light shining within her
will not fall on dirty places. She's living in
the light, following Jesus.

New Life

Therefore, if anyone is in Christ, he is a new creation; old things have passed away; behold, all things have become new.

2 CORINTHIANS 5:17 NKJV

———

New life in Christ: What indescribable freedom to be separated from our sin! No longer bound by it but able to live in Him, we joyfully race into our new existence. But in time, our tendency to fall into sin tarnishes God's gift. Suddenly we don't feel so new. "Old" Christians need only turn again to Christ for forgiveness, and the Spirit's cleansing makes us new again.

Celebrate Your Newness

*If Christ is in you, the body is dead because of sin,
but the Spirit is life because of righteousness.*

ROMANS 8:10 NKJV

⟡

Know Jesus? Then your body and your
fleshly desires are less important than your
spirit. Because Jesus lives in you, sin has
no permanent claim on your life. Though it
tempts you and you may give in for a time, it
no longer has a firm grasp on all your days.
You can turn aside from it and dwell in your
Lord instead. Celebrate your newness in
Jesus: Live for Him today!

Obedience

You Are Valuable

Who can find a virtuous woman?
for her price is far above rubies.

PROVERBS 31:10 KJV

———

Are you a virtuous woman? If so, you are
truly valuable, no matter how unbelievers
criticize you. Proverbs 31 says you can have
a profitable life with good relationships, a
happy home life, and successful business
ventures, if you run your life according to
God's principles. So don't worry about the
opinions of others if they don't mesh with
God's. Instead, obey Him and be a
valuable jewel to your Lord.

Love and Obey

"Whoever has my commands and obeys them, he is the one who loves me."

JOHN 14:21

Do you feel you love God with all your heart? Then show it by obeying Him. Jesus paved the path for you. Through His own sacrificial life, He showed you what it means to obey the Father. A Christian who lives for herself, rather than God, shows wavering commitment. One who loves God wholeheartedly walks in Jesus' way, obeying His commands in scripture. Here is where we start: Love God? Then obey Him, too.

Blessings Will Come

"All these blessings shall come upon you and overtake you, because you obey the voice of the LORD your God."

DEUTERONOMY 28:2 NKJV

───◦◦◦───

Obey God; receive blessings. It seems simple enough, doesn't it? Then why do we obey and only get in more trouble than before? Perhaps it's because we're looking at it from our perspective, not His. Blessings do not always follow on the heels of obedience; they often take time to appear. Today's blessings may result from long-ago faithfulness. But because God has promised, we know good things come, if only we wait.

Into Eternity

Blessed are they that do his commandments, that
they may have right to the tree of life, and may
enter in through the gates into the city.

REVELATION 22:14 KJV

———

The blessings of obedience not only impact us today; they follow us into eternity.
Whatever we do to please God never dies.
By trusting in Jesus, the works that demon-
strate our faith give us joy now and remain
secure for the future in the One who never
changes. We look forward to life in the
New Jerusalem even as we reap
His blessings now.

Prayer

Prayer—Give and Receive

Brothers, pray for us.

1 THESSALONIANS 5:25

Do you find it hard to ask others to pray
for you? Don't be afraid to take that step
into humility. Paul wasn't, when he asked
the Thessalonians to pray for his ministry.
Being part of the church requires an inter-
dependence of prayers given and received.
As a congregation prays for each other, their
spirits connect in a new, caring way. Choose
carefully those with whom you share private
concerns, but never fear to ask a mature
Christian to pray for you.

The Best Answer

Pray without ceasing.

1 Thessalonians 5:17 KJV

⸺

Haven't gotten an answer to your prayer? Don't give up. There's no time limit on speaking to God about your needs. It's just that we often work on a different time schedule from God. We want an answer yesterday, while He has something better in mind for tomorrow. So keep praying. God listens to His children and gives them the best answer, not the fastest one.

God Hears

"Therefore I tell you, whatever you ask for in prayer, believe that you have received it, and it will be yours."

MARK 11:24

This verse is not prescribing some magical incantation, but faith that God hears and answers our requests. When we trust that He knows our needs and wants to respond to them, we are in a position to receive. Would Jesus be proud of our requests? Do we seek the good of others? Or do we look only to our own desires? God answers prayers that reflect His will. How do yours stack up against this measure?

Turn to Him

Rejoicing in hope, patient in tribulation,
continuing steadfastly in prayer.

When do you pray the most, in times of ease or trial? Like most folks, you probably bend God's ear when you're hurting physically or spiritually, and that makes sense. For who helps the way God does? Paul describes the Christian's best response to trouble in these pithy phrases. While the faithless might rail against God, complaining that He is unfair, Christians know otherwise. We have a hope, a reason for patience, and a Father who cares. Let's turn to Him, no matter what our need.

Love Your Enemy

*"But I tell you: Love your enemies and
pray for those who persecute you."*

MATTHEW 5:44

⌘

Without God's strength, could any of us
follow this command of Jesus for more than
a very brief time? Consistently loving an
enemy is a real challenge. If you hurt from
pain inflicted by another, you hardly want to
pray for her. But loving actions and prayer
can bring great peace between two people
at odds with each other. For those who
consistently follow this command,
strife may not last forever.

Healing Power

*The prayer of faith will save the sick, and
the Lord will raise him up. And if he has
committed sins, he will be forgiven.*

JAMES 5:15 NKJV

Have you seen the amazing healing power
of prayer? As faithful Christians lift a suf-
ferer up to God, He works in the body, but
also in the heart and soul. Know someone
who is ill? Pray for physical health to return. But don't forget to include spiritual
needs, for the Great Physician treats the
whole person. Some spiritual issue may
be the real problem that requires healing.

Prayer from the Heart

Some trust in chariots, and some in horses; but we will remember the name of the LORD our God.

PSALM 20:7 NKJV

⸺⸺⸺

This may seem an odd prayer for a king going out to battle, but it shows where David's heart was. He knew his war equipment could fail, but God could not. What danger can we face that God is incapable of defending us from? None. Where have we placed our trust—in Him or in worldly defenses?

Repentance

Overcoming the Sin Barrier

Godly sorrow brings repentance that leads to salvation and leaves no regret.

2 CORINTHIANS 7:10

—⁂—

Godly sorrow comes when we feel the pain of our own sins. As we recognize our own wrongdoing and know that our actions have hurt us, others, and even the heart of God, we reach the place to do something about it. We repent, and God offers His salvation. Has sin come between you and your Savior? Turn at once in sorrow and ask Him to make everything right in your heart and soul. You'll never be sorry you did.

Cleansing Spirit

I came not to call the righteous,
but sinners to repentance.

LUKE 5:32 KJV

Repentance isn't meant for "good people"
who only have "tiny" sins to confess. This
verse reminds us that no sin is too awful for
God to hear about it. God calls all who are
sinful—those who most need Him and have
the most to fear from His awesome holiness.
Each of us may hesitate to confess sins and
admit to wrongs that embarrass us. But we
are just the ones He calls. One moment of
repentance, and His Spirit cleanses our lives.

Blessing behind Repentance

"Repent, then, and turn to God, so that your sins may be wiped out, that times of refreshing may come from the Lord."

ACTS 3:19

When we consider repentance, we tend to think it's hard. That's only because we're shortsighted. Giving up sin may not appeal to our hardened hearts because we're not looking at the blessing set behind repentance. Yet as we turn from sin, we feel the refreshing breath of God's Spirit bringing new life to our lives. Then, does anything seem difficult?

Compassion to Others

"And if he sins against you seven times in a day,
and seven times in a day returns to you, saying,
'I repent,' you shall forgive him."

LUKE 17:4 NKJV

―――

When another offends us, do we pass on the
forgiveness we have received? That's what
Jesus commanded. Remembering how gracious God has been to us, we need to show it
to those who affront us, too. As we think of
our many sins that God put behind His back,
can we fail to show compassion to others?

Salvation

Available 24/7

"Blessed is the man to whom the
Lord shall not impute sin."

ROMANS 4:8 NKJV

Sin forgiven: What a wonderful thought! No longer do we need to be dragged into wrong-doing, because God has cleansed our hearts. His Spirit sweeps through us, lifting the burden of sin from our lives. Though we still fail, in Christ, God will not hold the sin against us. Forgiveness, available 24/7, sends His Spirit through our lives again and again.

Reconcilers

God was reconciling the world to himself in Christ, not counting men's sins against them. And he has committed to us the message of reconciliation.

2 CORINTHIANS 5:19

———∞∞∞———

The Lord loved you so much that He paid a huge price to draw you into His arms. Jesus' sacrifice destroyed the sin barrier that separates humanity and God. Those who repent are reconciled to their holy God. But faith does not stop there. He makes us reconcilers, too, as He sends us out with the message that has meant so much: "God loves you, too."

Saving Grace

My soul finds rest in God alone;
my salvation comes from him.

PSALM 62:1

∞

At the moment you repented of your sins
and asked Jesus to control your life, God
saved you. But He didn't stop there. Each
day of your life, He continues His saving work. He redirects you, protects you,
and provides for your every need. In any
trouble, rest in Him. He will not fail.

Shine for Him

*[Jesus] gave himself for us to redeem us from all
wickedness and to purify for himself a people that
are his very own, eager to do what is good.*

Titus 2:14

Is there any sin from which Jesus cannot
save us? No. As long as we look to Him, He
will lead us into increasing, joyous holiness.
God takes sinful people and changes their
lives, making them His hands in an evil
world. As His people draw near Him,
putting off sin, their good works shine forth
the nature of their Savior. Will you
shine for Him today?

Our Partner

*Continue to work out your salvation
with fear and trembling.*

PHILIPPIANS 2:12

⬧⬧⬧

Salvation is hard work! Not only did it require Jesus' crucifixion for our sins, but we have a part in the effort, too. We have to live out the commands in God's Word that make our faith have an impact on our world. But we need not feel discouraged, for we are not alone in the labor. God acts through us, by His Spirit. What better working partner could we have than God Himself?

The Glory of Jesus

*From the beginning God chose you to be saved. . .
He called you. . .that you might share in the glory
of our Lord Jesus Christ.*

2 THESSALONIANS 2:13–14

Did you know you share Jesus' glory? Not because you are doing a wonderful job as a Christian, but simply because He decided to call you to Himself. God chose to share Himself with you, and make you like His Son. Daily, He calls you to learn more of His magnificence as you faithfully follow Him. Isn't it wonderful to share just a bit of God's greatness?

Serving God

Spiritual Training

All Scripture. . .is useful for. . .training in righteousness, so that the man of God may be thoroughly equipped for every good work.

2 TIMOTHY 3:16–17

※

Did you realize that God prepares you to do good works every day of your life? Because you believe in Him, He will lead you to do good, following His plan for your life. How do you start? By reading the scriptures, His guidebook. There you will learn what to believe, how to act, and how to speak with love. Soon you'll be ready to put into action all you've learned.

Serving Others

*You. . .were called to be free. But do not use
your freedom to indulge the sinful nature;
rather, serve one another in love.*

GALATIANS 5:13

⟨≋⟩

As women, we know a lot about serving:
We serve on many fronts and sometimes
wonder why this is our lot. God tells us He
freed us from sin, not to do what we like but
so we can share His love. If we're tempted to
fulfill our own sinful desires, let's remind
ourselves why we are here—we obey Jesus by
doing good for others. If that's not our goal,
we need redirection from Him.

You're Equipped

You have been given fullness in Christ, who is the head over every power and authority.

COLOSSIANS 2:10

❦

Do you feel incomplete or inadequate, unable to carry out the tasks God has given you? You aren't, you know, if you tap into His Spirit. God equips you to do all things in Him. If you feel overwhelmed, make sure you haven't taken on tasks rightfully belonging to someone else. God does not overload your life with busyness. He has a purpose for all you do. So be certain you're serving in the right place, doing the work He planned for you.

Make the Most

*Since everything will be destroyed in this way,
what kind of people ought you to be? You
ought to live holy and godly lives.*

2 Peter 3:11

⊷∞⊶

Knowing that the world will not last forever,
how should we act? We have no devil-may-
care option, in which we act as if eternity
did not matter, because God calls us to live
wholly for Him. The world's destruction
should not make us careless, but vigilant to
make the most of our time. In the end,
all we do here will not be lost but will
pass on into eternity.

Spiritual Gifts

You Have Gifts!

Now to each one the manifestation of the Spirit is given for the common good.

1 CORINTHIANS 12:7

Did you know that you are a gifted person? God gives each of His children spiritual gifts designed to help themselves and others—wisdom, knowledge, faith, healing, to name just a few. As you grow spiritually, you begin to unwrap those presents from God. Over time, you may be surprised and blessed at how many He's provided for you. Feeling unimportant? Remind yourself that you're gifted by God!

Grace Is a Gift

*But unto every one of us is given grace according
to the measure of the gift of Christ.*

EPHESIANS 4:7 KJV

⸻

We don't usually think of grace as a "spiritual gift." But consider: It's the basis for all the gifts God gives us. Without His gracious forgiveness, we'd have nothing spiritually. Our sins so separate us, that only His forgiveness allows us to approach Him. Whether we receive a large measure of grace or a smaller one, it is the perfect gift, given by Jesus, just for us. Let's appreciate what it cost Him and walk in Him today.

For His Glory

*We have different gifts, according
to the grace given us.*

ROMANS 12:6

❦

Your spiritual gifts are tailored especially
for you. God has a purpose for your life. To
help you accomplish it, He has given just the
gifts you need—nothing more, nothing less.
Doesn't knowing that God has gifted you
in just the right way make you feel special?
Thank Him for those gifts today, and
use them for the glory of His kingdom
and to help others.

Reach Out

Try to excel in gifts that build up the church.

1 Corinthians 14:12

———

Paul's words to the Corinthians were meant
for us, too. We should build up the church,
not ourselves, through our spiritual gifts.
When God gave you a special combination of
spiritual abilities, it wasn't to make you feel
important. He designed them to help you
reach out to those who need to accept Him
as Savior and to support believers who also
have your mission to reach the world. Is that
how you're using your gifts today?

Strength

In His Power

*I can do all things through Christ
who strengthens me.*

PHILIPPIANS 4:13 NKJV

———

Need strength? Turn to God for all you
need. Why take on life by yourself, when
He offers all you need? Often, as obedient Christians, we make great efforts
with our feeble spiritual muscles. But
ultimately, our own strength always fails.
When Christ's Spirit works through us, the
Christian life flows smoothly; in His power
we accomplish His purposes. Today, is
Christ bearing the burden, or are we? Only
He has the might we need in our lives.

Christian Strength

*Finally, be strong in the Lord
and in his mighty power.*

EPHESIANS 6:10

—∞∞—

When you rely on God's strength, what are
you tapping into? Not some small pool of
power that fails at a critical moment. The
Christian's strength is mighty, because God
is mighty. He who created the universe does
not have a short arm that cannot reach down
to your situation. Shining stars testify to His
authority. Galaxies in space are ordered by
His hand. Cannot He order your life, too?
Ask Him to use His strength in your life, and
you will have all you need.

Have Courage

*Be on your guard; stand firm in the faith;
be men of courage; be strong.*

1 Corinthians 16:13

Being a Christian can take lots of courage. As the world around us becomes increasingly hostile to God and our personal lives become tense because of our beliefs, we feel the challenge. But we are not defenseless. Christians through the ages have faced these troubles and triumphed. The Lord who supported them gives us strength, too. Let us stand fast for Jesus, calling on His Spirit to strengthen our lives. Then, we will be strong indeed.

Uplift Others

*We who are strong ought to bear with the failings
of the weak and not to please ourselves.*

ROMANS 15:1

⸻

So God has made you strong in some area—
perhaps by experience, as you have strug-
gled to obey Him. Now, how do you respond
to others? Don't criticize those who have
different experiences or other strengths, or
carp about the failings of new, weak Christians. Instead, use your power to uplift others. Come alongside and help. Then God's
strength will have helped you both.

Seek His Strength

Our sufficiency is from God.

2 Corinthians 3:5 NKJV

⸻

Feel unable to take on life? Paul knows how you feel. He didn't see himself as the perfect apostle we often think him. Knowing his own flaws and failures, Paul recognized the work Jesus did in him every day. God made His servant sufficient to his tasks. He'll do it for you, too, as you walk in faith and seek His strength.

Success

You Will Prosper

*"But you shall meditate in it [the Book of the Law]
day and night. . .do not turn from it. . .
that you may prosper."*

JOSHUA 1:7–8 NKJV

———

God promised success to Joshua, if he
obeyed His Word. That promise works for
you, too. But sometimes you may not feel
that obeying God has brought you great
prosperity. Just wait. It may take time, the
success may not take the form you expect,
or you may not see the results until you
reach heaven, but God will prosper those
who do His will. He promised it,
and His promises never fail.

Eternal Blessings

A faithful man will abound with blessings, but he who hastens to be rich will not go unpunished.

PROVERBS 28:20 NKJV

Faithfulness to God or success in the world:
Have you had to choose between them?
Seeking the world's goals brings short-term
benefits, but only God provides abundant
and ongoing blessings for those who put
serving Him first in their lives. Though
worldly blessings last for a day, a year, or a
few years, they cannot remain for eternity.
When you consider success, think of the
kind that really lasts.

Living in Him

*The meek will inherit the land
and enjoy great peace.*

PSALM 37:11

—❧—

You might call this God's definition of success: a profitable land that provides for His people and His peace that provides a blessed life. Notice that money and other possessions aren't mentioned. But the peace of living in Him flows freely to those who abide in Him. Would this be success to you? If not, what does it tell you about your spiritual life?

Real Success

*Save now, we beseech You, O Lord; send now
prosperity, O Lord, we beseech You,
and give to us success!*

PSALM 118:25 AMP

Is it wrong to pray for success? No. But
notice that the Bible connects success to
God's salvation. Prosperity or any other
achievement means little when it's separated from God's will and our obedience to
Him. When you ask to attain something, do
you also seek God's saving grace in that part
of your life? If so, you'll have real success—
spiritual and temporal blessings.

Temptation

Escape Hatch

No temptation has seized you except what is common to man. And God is faithful. . .when you are tempted, he will also provide a way out so that you can stand up under it.

1 CORINTHIANS 10:13

∞

No matter how powerful it seems, you need not give in to temptation. God always provides you with an escape hatch. When temptation pulls at you, turn your eyes to Jesus. Replace that tempting object with Him, and you will not fall.

Ask Jesus

Because he himself suffered when he was tempted,
he is able to help those who are being tempted.

HEBREWS 2:18

Why can Jesus help us when temptation
strikes? Because He's walked a mile in our
shoes. He knows how strongly sin attracts
us. But because He never fell prey to it,
He can effectively show us how to resist
even the strongest enticement. The biggest
mistakes we make are not calling on Him
and not persistently seeking His powerful
aid, when Satan repeatedly lures us into sin.
Need help? Just ask Jesus.

Lean on Jesus

*"Therefore if the Son makes you free,
you shall be free indeed."*

JOHN 8:36 NKJV

———

Sometimes we don't feel freed from sin.
Temptations draw us, even though we
love Jesus. So His words here can be both
comforting and challenging. The Jews
wanted to trust in their spiritual history,
not God. That plan didn't work well for
them, and it won't work for us, either.
We can't rely on history or our past deeds
to put sin behind us. What will work?
Leaning on Jesus every day, trusting Him
to make us free indeed!

God Is Greater

Each one is tempted when, by his own evil desire, he is dragged away and enticed.

JAMES 1:14

⸛⸛⸛

God does not draw us into temptation. He is holy, unable to tempt anyone into wrongdoing. The attraction for sin comes from within us, because our evil desires lead us toward sin. When we face situations that encourage our own wickedness, they are not designed by God to make us fall. Instead, they provide opportunities to turn to Him and progressively turn away from iniquity. No evil within us is so great that God is not greater still.

God's Protection

The Lord knows how to deliver the godly out of
temptations and to reserve the unjust under
punishment for the day of judgment.

2 PETER 2:9 NKJV

⸺◦◦◦⸺

Feeling surrounded by temptations? God
hasn't forgotten you. He knows how to protect His children from harm and offers His
wisdom to His children. Maybe you need to
avoid places that could lead you into sin—that
may mean taking action like finding a new
job or new friends. When God is trying to
protect you, don't resist. Sin is never better
than knowing Him.

Thankfulness

Give Thanks

Give thanks to the God of gods.
His love endures forever.

PSALM 136:2

Having trouble being thankful? Read Psalm 136. You'll be reminded of the wonders of God's power and His enduring love. The God who protected Israel watches over you, too. Even when there may be little in your life to rejoice about, you can always delight in Him. Give thanks to God. He has not forgotten you—His love endures forever.

God Saves

I will give you thanks, for you answered me;
you have become my salvation.

PSALM 118:21

———

A new believer didn't write this verse. The
psalmist thanks God not just for loving Him
enough to tear Him from the claws of origi-
nal sin; instead, this mature man of faith
recognizes that God saves him every day,
whenever he is in trouble. God does this in
your life, too. What salvation has He worked
in your life recently? What thanks do you
need to offer Him now?

Eternal Appreciation

O LORD my God, I will give you thanks forever.

PSALM 30:12

—⦿—

Even in eternity, you will be thanking God. The appreciation of God's mercy by His people never stops. Without His grace, we would be forever separated from Him, lost in the cares of sin and a hellish existence. The bliss of a heavenly eternity could not be our inheritance. Could you thank Jesus too much now? Or could you ever find enough words to show Him your love? Maybe it's time to get started on your eternal appreciation of your Lord.

Appreciation Overflow

Continue to live in [Jesus], rooted and built up in him, strengthened in the faith as you were taught, and overflowing with thankfulness.

COLOSSIANS 2:6–7

Strong Christians are thankful Christians. As we realize all Jesus has sacrificed for us and appreciate our inability to live the Christian life on our own, we remember to praise our Savior for His grace. Today, we can be rooted in Jesus, strong in our faith, and thankful to the One who has given us these blessings. Let's overflow with appreciation!

Wonderful Thanks

Oh, give thanks to the LORD, for He is good!
For His mercy endures forever.

PSALM 136:1 NKJV

—◈◈◈—

Now, honestly, how do you respond to this
call for thanks? Does your heart leap at the
opportunity, or does it just hit you with a
dull thud? Why is it so important to thank
God? Because He will always be merciful to
you. Whether you rejoice easily or hit the
floor with a thud, if you have trusted in the
Savior, He still loves you. Isn't that something wonderful to give thanks for?

Troubles

God Calls Us to Joy

Consider it pure joy, my brothers,
whenever you face trials of many kinds.

JAMES 1:2

Joy? To be faced with trials should cause us joy? Hard to imagine, isn't it? But God calls us to joy when unbelievers persecute us because of our faith or when our situation is merely difficult. It is a joy to Him that we have stood firm in faith, and He calls us to share His delight. That doesn't mean we seek out trials but that we face the situation hand in hand with God. In trials, our spiritual strength increases.

Look Ahead to Heaven

*For our light and momentary troubles
are achieving for us an eternal glory
that far outweighs them all.*

2 CORINTHIANS 4:17

———

What trouble could you face on earth
that will not seem small in heaven? No
pain from this life will impede you there.
Blessing for faithful service to God will
replace each heartache that discourages
you today. When trials and troubles beset
you, look ahead to heaven. Jesus promises
you an eternal reward, if you keep
your eyes on Him.

Joy Is Straight Ahead

The genuineness of your faith, being much more precious than gold that perishes, though it is tested by fire, may be found to praise, honor, and glory at the revelation of Jesus Christ.

1 PETER 1:7 NKJV

———

Trials have a purpose in our lives. As a smith heats up gold to purify it, God heats up our lives to make spiritual impurities rise to the surface. If we cooperate with Him, sin is skimmed off our lives, purifying our faith. Cleansed lives bring glory to God and joy to us. If a trial lies before you today, envision the joy ahead.

Hope in God Alone

Because of the LORD's great love we are not consumed, for his compassions never fail.

LAMENTATIONS 3:22

———

Despite his deep troubles, as Jeremiah sorrowed over Judah's exile, hope remained in his heart. Though he and his nation faced terrible trials, the prophet understood that God would still uphold them. God's compassion never fails His hurting people. No matter how we struggle, we share the prophet's hope. God alone comforts our hearts as we stumble along a rocky trail.

His Concern

The righteous cry out, and the Lord hears,
and delivers them out of all their troubles.

PSALM 34:17 NKJV

—◦◦◦—

As God's child, you have His ear 24/7, if only
you will pray. Every need, trouble, or praise
is His concern. And not only will He hear
about your trials, He will deliver you from
them. Feel discouraged in your troubles?
You need not stay that way. Just spend time
with Jesus. His help is on the way.

Wisdom

Wisdom in God

Wisdom is the principal thing; therefore get wisdom: and with all thy getting get understanding.

PROVERBS 4:7 KJV

~~~

Have you ever thought of yourself as wise?
The Bible says you can be. You don't need
a lot of education or a certain IQ. Real
wisdom is found in God. Simply obey
your Lord's commandments and make
knowing Him well your first priority.
Seek after wisdom, and you will find it in
Him. As you daily search for truth in the
Word, your understanding grows.

Greater Ways

For since, in the wisdom of God, the world through wisdom did not know God, it pleased God through the foolishness of the message preached to save those who believe.

1 CORINTHIANS 1:21 NKJV

———

To this world, God's wisdom doesn't look very wise. Anyone who denies Jesus is blind to the depth of insight God showed in sending His Son to die for us and then raising Him from the dead. But those who accept His sacrifice understand that God's ways are greater than ours and His astuteness far outweighs our own. As His wisdom fills our once-foolish lives, we gain a new perspective on His perception.

Wise Humility

Woe unto them that are wise in their own eyes,
and prudent in their own sight!

ISAIAH 5:21 KJV

***

Wisdom without humility isn't wisdom
at all. When we feel astute under our own
power, we are actually in big trouble and
are heading into foolishness! The truly wise
person recognizes that all wisdom comes
from God, not frail humans. As we tap into
His mind and connect with His astuteness,
we are wise indeed. There is no one
wiser than He.

Wise Words

She speaks with wisdom, and faithful instruction is on her tongue.

PROVERBS 31:26

The virtuous woman's mouth speaks kindly wisdom. Hers is no sharp tongue that destroys relationships. As we seek to do God's will, truthful yet caring speech must be ours. Wise words heal hurting hearts. If we have trouble knowing what words bring God's healing, we need only to ask Him to let His Spirit bring wisdom and kindness to our mouths and tongues. When we speak as His Spirit directs, we are wise indeed.

Seek Counsel

The way of a fool is right in his own eyes,
but he who heeds counsel is wise.

PROVERBS 12:15 NKJV

——◆——

Listening to others who are wise brings
us wisdom, too. Before we make serious
choices, we need to seek the counsel
of others. How can we recognize the wise
ones? Those who have experience, faith,
and who have made decisions that blessed
their lives can pass their wisdom on to us,
too. Is there some wise person you need
to consult now?

Witness

Shine On

"You are the light of the world.
A city on a hill cannot be hidden."

<small>MATTHEW 5:14</small>

❈

God means you to be a light set where the
world can see it clearly—not a hidden flame
behind closed doors, with curtains drawn.
Being a light isn't always easy—people see
everything you do, and they don't always like
it. Don't let the critics stop you. Your works
were ordained to glorify God, not make
people comfortable. Knowing that, are you
ready to shine today?

Share His Love

I pray that you may be active in sharing your faith,
so that you will have a full understanding of every
good thing we have in Christ.

PHILEMON 1:6

Many of us have a hard time sharing our
faith. So when we hear Paul's encouragement to Philemon, our hearts lift, knowing
we aren't the only ones who struggle. Isn't
the challenge of witnessing to others worth
it, once we've read this promise? The salvation of others and our own appreciation of
our Lord: Could we have better reasons
to share His love?

Kind Words

Let your speech always be with grace, seasoned with salt, that you may know how you ought to answer each one.

COLOSSIANS 4:6 NKJV

❦

Your words are a vital part of your witness. Speak to an unbeliever ungraciously, and chances are good that she will never forget it. But study and grow in the Word; then speak wisely and generously to others, and God can use your words to win them to His kingdom. People respond well to kindness and flavorful speech. What are your words saying today?

Turn from Wrong

There is therefore now no condemnation to those who are in Christ Jesus, who do not walk according to the flesh, but according to the Spirit.

ROMANS 8:1 NKJV

※

No condemnation! What a wonderful thought for sinners! Forgiven, we know the comfort of having heaven as our ultimate destination. But have we also read the second part of the verse? This is no blanket agreement that okays sin. The joy of our freedom must lead us to turn from all wrong. Our Lord gives the strength to grow in Him.

God's Compassionate Salvation

Do not repay anyone evil for evil. Be careful to do what is right in the eyes of everybody.

ROMANS 12:17

❧

Tit-for-tat retribution for evil is not a principle of our compassionate God. We understand this if we've received His undeserved salvation. With such a gift, God has opened our hearts to treating our enemies as He has treated us. If we fail to count up each wrong and repay it with harshness, lost souls may understand God's compassionate salvation. By doing right, even when we receive wrong in return, we become powerful witnesses.

Live Out Forgiveness

*Be kind and compassionate to one another, forgiving
each other, just as in Christ God forgave you.*

EPHESIANS 4:32

⸺※⸺

Because all Christians are forgiven sinners,

not perfect people, the need for forgiveness

does not stop at the church door. So Paul

calls us not only to live out compassion to

the world, but within our congregations, as

well. As we set aside anger and other harsh

attitudes, we live out the forgiveness all

believers have received. Is there any better

way to share His love?

Work

Inheritors of Earth

"Blessed are the meek,
for they will inherit the earth."

MATTHEW 5:5

In the workplace, meekness isn't often seen
as a positive thing. "Looking out for number
one" is the theory of many who tout asser-
tiveness as the way to get the most out of life.
But God doesn't say that. Ultimately, those
who follow Him faithfully and show their
belief to the world will not be the "nice
guys" who "finish last," but the inheritors of
this earth. What plot of earth might God
have mapped out for you?

Everything for God

Whatever you do, work at it with all your heart,
as working for the Lord.

COLOSSIANS 3:23

⸺◦⸺

Did you know you are not really working
for your boss? Yes, you report to the one
whom your company hired in that position, but ultimately, you do everything
for God, not a man or woman. So even if
your boss isn't great to work for, remind
yourself that you are accountable to Jesus.
No matter who has the position above
yours, your Lord is always in charge of
your future.

Serious Business

*Make it your ambition to lead a quiet life, to mind
your own business and to work with your hands.*

1 Thessalonians 4:11

⸺⸺

Whether we work at a computer or on a fac-
tory production line, those of us who work
with our hands shouldn't feel unimportant.
Manual labor is serious business in God's
sight. Christians who quietly, faithfully
go about their business day by day make
an important contribution, bearing God's
message to a wide range of people. What a
testimony our lives become, when we live
out this verse.

God's Favor

May the favor of the Lord our God rest upon us;
establish the work of our hands for us.

PSALM 90:17

∞

Want your work to be effective? Don't make
sure the boss knows every good thing you
do. Seek God's favor, and He will see to
it that your work really gets the job done,
whether you're caring for a child, arguing
a legal case, or waiting on a customer. Our
Lord makes His people productive for Him
as they serve others in His name.

Worldliness

No Compromises

Do not love the world or anything in the world.
If anyone loves the world, the love of the
Father is not in him.

1 JOHN 2:15

This verse is likely to hit us right where we
live. The world's way tempts us more than
we'd like to admit. But when we feel the pull
of worldliness, do we remember that we're
actually making a larger decision about loving
God? Gaining the small, temporal things is
not worth compromising our faith. Let's save
our love for the One who really deserves it.

More Than Temporary

*Do not be afraid when one becomes rich,
when the glory of his house is increased; for
when he dies he shall carry nothing away;
his glory shall not descend after him.*

PSALM 49:16–17 NKJV

———

This is the Bible's way of saying, "You can't take it with you." When life ends, the only treasures that remain are the works we have done for Jesus. Money and fame cling to earth, soon to be forgotten. So when unbelievers seem to get all the goodies, we just remember that the treasures we send ahead to heaven are greater than any temporary gain.

Belong to Jesus

"If you belonged to the world, it would love you as its own. As it is, you do not belong to the world, but I have chosen you out of the world. That is why the world hates you."

JOHN 15:19

———

Don't expect the world to love you for loving Jesus. Because He doesn't accept its evil, and neither do you, the world is at enmity with both of you. That's not such a bad thing. Who would you rather belong to: Jesus, who holds eternity's joys in His hands, or the world, which offers so much sin and pain?

Kingdom-Purposed Friendship

"I tell you, use worldly wealth to gain friends for yourselves, so that when it is gone, you will be welcomed into eternal dwellings."

LUKE 16:9

—∞—

There is a good way to use the things of the world, and Jesus describes it here. God has given us the wealth to share with others, making use of it to further God's kingdom. Though we may not have more than a pot of soup and some bread to offer, they can be the start of a kingdom-purposed friendship. What have you got that God can use this way?

Notes

Notes

Notes

Notes

Notes

Notes

Notes

Notes

Notes